Jumpin' Jake Settles Down

A Workbook to Help Impulsive Children Learn To Think Before They Act

By Lawrence E. Shapiro, Ph.D.

Illustrated by Reggie Byers

Childswork Childsplay

Plainview, New York

Jumpin' Jake Settles Down

By Lawrence E. Shapiro, Ph.D.
Illustrated by Reggie Byers

Childswork/Childsplay publishes products for mental health professionals, teachers, and parents who wish to help children with their developmental, social and emotional growth. For questions, comments, or to request a free catalog describing hundreds of games, toys, books, and other counseling tools, call 1-800-962-1141.

© 1994 Childswork/Childsplay, LLC
A Guidance Channel Company
135 Dupont Street
Plainview, NY 11803

All rights reserved.
Printed in the United States of America

ISBN 1-882732-11-1

Helping Impulsive Children

Impulsivity in children surfaces in many forms. There is the impulsive child who studies hard, but guesses at the answer on his history quiz and receives a poor grade. There is the impulsive child who is easily influenced by his peers and does things which he knows are wrong without regard to the consequences. And then there are the tens of thousands of children who are diagnosed with Attention Deficit Disorders (ADD) who seem to always be doing and saying things without thinking them through—to the amazement and chagrin of the adults around them.

Impulsivity appears to be a cognitive "style," present in some children in infancy, just as reflection and introspection appears to be an inborn characteristic of other children.

Unlike other children of the same age, impulsive children tend to rely less on specific kinds of thought patterns, including: planning ahead, identifying and weighing alternatives, and foreseeing the consequences of one's actions. When faced with a decision, they rely on intuition, the "feel" of the situation, or just plain trial and error. We frequently see these children making the same mistakes over and over again, because they do not seem to integrate the many threads of their experiences into a fabric of common logic.

A variety of studies have suggested that the typical impulsive child is *capable* of these higher forms of thinking, but for whatever reason s/he does not use them to direct his/her behaviors. The theory of cognitive-behavior modification suggests that impulsive children can *learn* to "think before they act," *if* they have sufficient practice in using these cognitive skills, and *if* these skills are in turn reinforced in the real world.

This book of activities was designed to give impulsive children a variety of challenging games and puzzles to help stimulate their cognitive resources. In addition, we hope that it will help make children *and* adults aware that impulsivity is a problem that can be addressed as an issue distinct from one's behaviors. Children may sometimes make the wrong choices as a result of their impulsivity, but this does not make them "bad" kids. All children eventually grow up and learn to control or adapt to their natural inclination toward impulsive behavior.

When they are grown, we hope that these children will have learned a foundation of values on which to make their decisions and that they will remember their childhood as a time when thoughtful adults gave them support and guidance.

Jake the Jump Frog was a troublin' kind of swamp frog.

He came from a nice family of responsible goin'-to-work-type frogs, who watched the evening news every night at six, and ate their flies with a knife and fork, and generally speaking, were as quiet and regular folks as frogs can be.

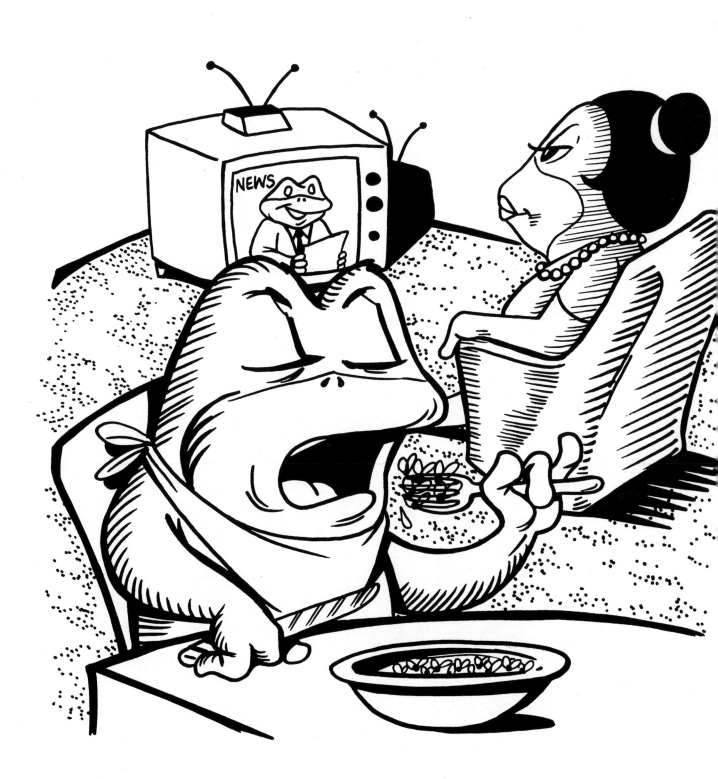

But Jumpin' Jake was an itchin' kind of frog.

He was always itchin' to be outside hoppin' about to and fro.

Or itchin' to be off with his gang of Mack the Mongoose and Vance the Viper, who every day seemed hide-and-skin bent on rilin' up folks with all sorts of antics, like puttin' eggs in critters' pants, and unscrewin' all the lids on the jars in the refrigerator, or droolin' spit over the railing of the balcony at the library.

Jake was pretty much always itchin' to just do as he pleased.

That's not to say that Jake was a bad kind of frog, 'cause he had a good heart, and a good mind, too.

If he saw an old frog with his tongue snagged on a briar bush, 'cause he missed at trying to catch one of them fast sassy-type flies for dinner, Jake would go over and pull that old bull frog's tongue off the briars and even pick the briars out of his tongue, with nary a look of "you sure are a slow old kind of ugly frog."

But rather, Jake would give a kind of respectful-type "I hope this doesn't hurt" croak as he jumped over the old bull frog and the briar bush.

The swamp critters would often say that if Jake could just slow himself down a mite, he could be some-kind-of-a-special-type frog, and maybe even grow up to be the mayor of the swamp.

But it didn't really look like that was goin' to happen. Why should it?

There were plenty of itchin'-type frogs that itched and hopped themselves right into Hunter McAllister's big net and ended up the wrong-side-down in somebody's frog-and-tater soup.

And there were plenty of itchin'-type frogs that hopped themselves right to the County Jail, or the Home for Wayward Frogs, or just the No Place Special, which was right around the corner from Goin' Nowhere Fast.

Jake was a special type of determined frog and wanted to make his parents proud. And you can help him. Do all the activities in this book and you'll see where Jake ends up!

Jake wanted to slow down, but it wasn't his natural way. His teacher wrote down some words that would help Jake remember to take things a little slower. Can you find these words or phrases in the swamp?

SLOW   EASY DOES IT   THINK FIRST   CALM

PLAN AHEAD   TAKE YOUR TIME   RELAX

R S T I L F E A S Z O E C A
N I A O P O G C N E R T S E
G A K C A B R E L A X Q U T
I R E N A L V U T S S R Q S
Z O Y S L O W E D Y F N G M
A B O E L F X A B D G I K A
Y C U C D E Y Z C O T H E J
X E R P L A N A H E A D H I
Z T T K F Z O W K S Y I W X
P Q I L C D R O I I S T U V
O S M N B A E B P T M E Y S
M J E V R V L U B Q N P W A
E H S O L O P M L S E O I D
D F T H I N K F I R S T O R
B Q T S E I N O T A L F M M

Jake thought maybe he should avoid things that would distract him and keep him from doing his homework. Can you complete the maze by avoiding Jake's temptations?

Jake couldn't help but get into trouble sometimes. When he did, his mother said it would help to say he was sorry with a little present. One time, by accident, Jake spilled milk all over Grandpa's newspaper and Grandpa had nothing to read all day.

Can you think of something that Jake could make out of the materials he had around the house that would make Grandpa feel better?

Draw it if you can.

Jake also thought that maybe he should think more about others and less about himself and that would make him become a better frog. He made a calendar and wrote down all the birthdays of his friends and relatives. Here's a calendar like Jake's that you can use to write down the birthdays that you should remember.

BIRTHDAY CALENDAR

JANUARY		FEBRUARY		MARCH		APRIL	
DATE	NAME	DATE	NAME	DATE	NAME	DATE	NAME

MAY		JUNE		JULY		AUGUST	
DATE	NAME	DATE	NAME	DATE	NAME	DATE	NAME

SEPTEMBER		OCTOBER		NOVEMBER		DECEMBER	
DATE	NAME	DATE	NAME	DATE	NAME	DATE	NAME

Jake knew that he had a pretty bad temper. And when he got upset his mind went kind of blank. So he thought, "Maybe if I can figure out what upsets me, then I can avoid those things."

Write down the things that make you upset, either a little or a lot.

IRRITATED =

ANNOYED =

ANGRY =

REALLY STEAMED =

READY TO EXPLODE =

When the 'old' Jake did his homework, his mind would think about just about anything at all. But the 'new' Jake would think about something special when he did his homework, which helped him to work hard even when he didn't really feel like it. Draw in what you think the 'old Jake' and the 'new Jake' would think about.

Jake read a book that would help him relax when he got all tense and itchin'. Write down what the book's advice was. If you're not sure, ask a grown-up. (The answers are on page 55).

It wasn't too long before Jake's family started to notice a change in him. In this picture, see if you can find the things that Jake did that got him into trouble. Then, in the bottom picture, find the things he did that pleased his family. (The answers are on page 55.)

As the days went on Jake found that his itchin' got him into less and less trouble, but there were still some times that he had a slip-up or two. He found that when he did make a mistake, it helped to write an "I'm Sorry" note. He found it easier to make one card and then make copies and fill in the blank space when needed. How would you fill out your "I'm Sorry" card?

I'm Sorry?...

TO _____

I'M SORRY
FOR _____
_____
_____
_____

TO MAKE IT
UP I'LL _____
_____
_____
_____

SIGNED _____

Jake's mom made a chores chart to help remind Jake to do things around the house. Here's the chart that Jake used. You can use it to fill in the chores you do around your house.

CHORES CHART

CHART	TO DO	DONE
		CHECK OFF
MONDAY		
TUESDAY		
WEDNESDAY		
THURSDAY		
FRIDAY		
SATURDAY		
SUNDAY		

Jake also found it easier to get his homework done if he wrote down his assignments. Here's the assignment paper that Jake used. You can use it to keep track of your homework.

TO DO - TODAY

DAY _____ DATE _____

WHAT TO DO	WHAT I'LL NEED	WHEN TO DO IT	FINISHED - CHECKED BY: (TEACHER OR PARENT)
1.			
2.			
3.			
4.			
5.			
6.			

One bad habit that Jake tried hard to get rid of was making up excuses. When something went wrong, he tended to add a few details that weren't exactly true. Like one day, Jake didn't turn in his homework. Cross out the things that you think didn't really happen. (The answers are on page 55).

Once Jake had a very important homework assignment. His teacher said that it had to be really neat, or he would get a bad grade. Jake really wanted a good grade, but he had a tendency to hand in work that was pretty messy. Can you help him out? List all the things on Jake's desk which shouldn't be there and what could happen. (The answers are on page 55).

Now draw in the things that you think Jake should have on his desk.

Jake needed to control his temper. Pop Weasel, who had been in a bit of trouble himself when he was younger, told Jake that when he was angry, he should count to 10 before saying anything.

But Jake had a hard time remembering to count to 10, so Pop's advice really wasn't that helpful. Jake would say to himself,

TEN, TEN, TEN. I MUST REMEMBER TO COUNT TO TEN. IF THERE WAS JUST SOMETHING I COULD THINK OF THAT WOULD REMIND ME.

Can you help Jake remember to count to 10? Find all of the expressions that refer to 10 in the picture below. (The answers are on page 55).

Judge Phineas Frogbottom was one of the great thinkers of the swamp. He always had the right solution for every problem. Unfortunately, the Judge went on vacation for two-and-a-half weeks. Pretend you're the Judge and write in a solution to the following problems:

Jay and Paul Gator were two brothers who could never get along. They always fought over their toys. How would the Judge deal with their constant fighting?

_____

_____

Marcy Mouse was caught cheating on her spelling test. She had the answers pinned to her tail. How would the wise Judge help Marcy see the problems that can occur when you cheat?

_____

_____

Rinko the Rat was a total slob and drove his mother crazy because he wouldn't keep his rat's nest tidy. What would the Judge do to encourage Rinko to be neater?

_____

_____

23

Changing isn't easy for a hoppin' frog like Jake. There were many days when Jake would have rather played the day away rather than get to school on time. Of course, it didn't help when someone like Wendel Fox was around to tempt Jake into mischief. Can you help Jake get to school on time with this simple game?

You will need a ruler and a penny. Hold the ruler by the number "12" with the hand that you use to hold your pencil or pen. Now stretch your arm as high as it will go and let go of the ruler, catching it with your other hand. When you catch it, see what number your thumb is closest to. That's the number of spaces you can move ahead.

Now take a penny and place it at the beginning of Jake's path to school. Move the penny one web print for each number that comes up on the ruler. If you want to play against someone else, they can use a dime and you can race to the end.

GO BACK 2 SPACES

36 SWAMP LN.

HOME

START

This picture of Jake's living room doesn't look like a battleground, does it? But it is. There is a war for Jake's attention going on here. Put an "X" over the enemy: anything that will keep Jake from settling down and being a good student. Put a circle around the good guys: anything that will help Jake be more organized and on time. (The answers are on page 55).

Sometimes Jake had to go to the store for his mother by going through a neighborhood with many temptations. He'd go by Jennie the Goose's house, and he'd want to stop and play. Or there was the arcade, where he knew he would find Alice and Marvin Mosquito (they were twins), who would always want him to play a game or two of Mortal Kumquat.

But Jake knew that he had to resist all hurdles (hurdles are something you have to get over, no matter what) and pick up the groceries. Can you do it too? Here's a game to test your skill at avoiding obstacles.

Take four paper clips and fold them like this, making "hurdles:"

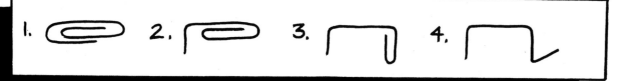

Now put the four "hurdles" on the table in front of you, spreading them out, and put one of the things that Jake has to pick up by each hurdle.

Cut out each of the six squares below and paste each one to a penny, and place each one by a hurdle.

To play the game you have to let your index finger and thumb walk to each hurdle, pick up the square, and step over the hurdle. There is only one catch...you have to do it with your eyes closed without knocking over any hurdles.

Stare at the hurdles before you start. Now go very slowly. Give yourself one point for each item you pick up without knocking over a hurdle.

Variation: Have another person guide you while your eyes remain shut, by saying, "right," "left," "forward," etc.

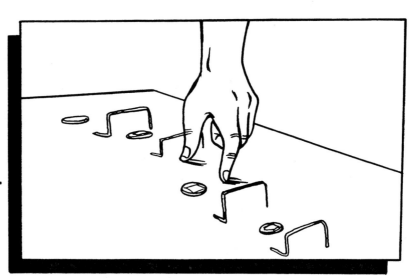

Jake had to go to the library for a dictionary, but he couldn't jump over a big tree that had fallen down. Can you find things in the picture that he could use to get over the tree? Use your imagination. (The answers are on page 55).

How creative are you at solving a problem like the one that Jake just had? Suppose you had to make a high tower on a table, but you could only use the things that could fit into your knapsack at the same time? Look around the room, or in your pocket, and make a tower as high as you can. You can use whatever objects you want as long as they can all fit in an average-sized knapsack. Here's how to score:

6 inch tower = 5 points
1 foot tower = 10 points
2 foot tower = 50 points

Jake's teacher got mad at him for being late coming in from recess. But Jake felt that it wasn't his fault and that it wasn't a big deal anyway. The "old" Jake would have made a face or stuck out his long tongue at the teacher. But the "new" Jake knew better—that he had to act respectful to his teacher. What did Jake say to himself to help him change his attitude and be more positive?

When Jake began to settle down, he suddenly found that he had more time to do things he had always wanted to try. He thought, "I think I'd like to start a hobby of collecting things, and put them in a neat case." But Jake couldn't think of what to collect. Can you look at this picture and find six common things that people collect? (The answers are on page 55).

When you are a hopping frog, it can be difficult to remember to slow down. It kind of goes against your grain. But Jake knew how important it was to slow down, nonetheless. So he invented a new way to play basketball, which he would do whenever he needed to remind himself to act a little slower (and to have some fun too!).

Did you ever play the game H-O-R-S-E? You have to make a basketball shot, and then the other player has to make the exact same shot or he/she gets a letter. The person who gets all five letters and spells "HORSE" first is the loser.

Jake made up a "basketball" game called S-L-O-W, which is played exactly like H-O-R-S-E except for the basket and the ball. Here's how to play: Use a paper cup as a "basket" and a nickel as a "ball." Set up a heavy book as a backboard. You make "shots" by flipping the coin into the cup. (Remember to take your time and go S-L-O-W).

When you are a young frog, even when you're trying to settle down, sometimes you do something wrong. Jake found out that there is one thing that you can say (when you really mean it) that always helps.

Unscramble the letters to see what Jake learned to say. (The answer is on page 55).

One day Jake was hopping along, minding his own business, when he tripped and fell into a pile of logs and boards. Patrick Rabbit came hopping along, and he told Jake that he would lift off everything to free his leg. But Jake said, "Be careful! If you lift the wrong thing, you could break my ankle!" Tell the order that the logs and boards should be lifted without causing the others to move (like the game "Pick-Up-Stix"). Mark each log or board with the correct number from one to five.

Jake found out that trying to change can be a lot easier when there is someone else to help. Match the person (or rather frog) who Jake got help from with the incomplete word below. (The answers are on page 55).

LET'S GO PLAY!

LET'S GO FISHING, SON.

I'M THE HEAD OF THE SCHOOL.

IT'S TIME FOR DINNER.

WANT SOME COOKIES?

HI, NEPHEW!

DO YOUR HOMEWORK.

1. __ e a __ __ e __

2. __ __ a n __ m __ __ __ __ __ __

3. F __ __ __ e __

4. __ __ i e __ __

5. P __ __ __ __ __ __ __ __ l

6. __ o __ __ __ r

7. u n __ __ __

Here's a game that is much easier when you have someone else to help. You will need eight pencils, a cup, two straws, and a small wad of paper. Arrange the pencils in a double zigzag and place the cup at the end, as pictured below. Now wad up a three-inch square of paper. Score a goal by blowing the paper around the square and into the cup. Since the air you blow through the straw can only go in one direction, you will find it much easier when both players cooperate, blowing on the paper simultaneously.

See how fast you can complete the maze without going outside the lines.

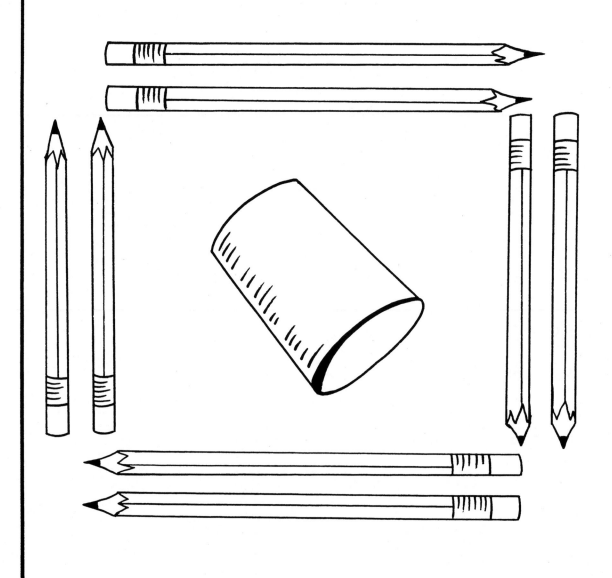

Jake found that to settle down he had a lot of bad habits he had to change. Can you look at his room and see some of the problems? (The answers are on page 55).

Can you think of some habits that you might want to change? Write
them below.

_____

_____

_____

When Jake used to get angry he'd get hoppin' mad. He'd get so hoppity he'd just hop himself right out the door and he never knew exactly just where he would land. But Jake learned something better to do when he was angry. Can you figure out what it was? (The answer is on page 55).

As hard as he tried, sometimes Jake just plumb broke the rules. Sometimes that happens to all kids and frogs. When Jake broke the rules he was punished. What punishment would you give for breaking the following rules? Write them below.

Not turning in homework _____

Forgetting to do chores _____

Coming in late for dinner _____

Lying _____

Hitting someone smaller _____

_____

Taking something that didn't belong to you

_____

_____

_____

As Jake learned to settle down, he found that a lot of his old friends weren't too happy about it. Sam the Snake, for example, couldn't understand why Jake didn't want to skip school and sneak into "R"-rated movies. Unfortunately for Jake, Sam was a very persuasive animal, and Jake had a hard time resisting him. One day, Jake's older brother Fred gave him some interesting advice. Fred said, "You just have to act like a broken record that keeps repeating itself. Think of something to say to Sam and just repeat it over and over again, no matter what Sam does. He'll stop, you'll see."

What do you think that Jake decided to say, over and over, to Sam?

Jake learned that he could do a lot better in school when he was organized. As it turned out, Jake found out that he loved organizing things! He also found out that there were many ways to organize and sort things. Can you think of five ways to organize or sort things? Take a look at Jake's room to help you think of some. (The answers are on page 55).

WRITE DOWN SOMETHING THAT YOU NEED TO ORGANIZE.

_____

WRITE DOWN THE NAME OF THE PERSON YOU KNOW WHO IS NOT ORGANIZED.

_____

WRITE DOWN SOMETHING THAT YOU THINK YOU SHOULD MAKE A LIST OF.

_____

IF SOMEONE COULD NEVER FIND THEIR HOMEWORK, HOW DO YOU THINK THEY COULD ORGANIZE THEMSELVES BETTER?

One day Jake hopped out of bed so fast that he hit his head on the ceiling. He felt so dizzy that he couldn't remember what to do first to get ready for school. Sort out the pictures below (number them 1 through 6) and show the order in which Jake should do things. (The answer is on page 55).

Sometimes it's important to think quickly, and at other times it is important to think slowly and carefully. Circle the situations where Jake should think slowly, and put an "X" on the situations where he should think quickly. (The answers are on page 55).

Nobody's perfect. As Jake worked hard at settling down, he sometimes made mistakes and sometimes had setbacks. What do you think he should say to himself when he feels discouraged?

What are three things that you can do to help you when you are discouraged?

1. _____

   _____

2. _____

   _____

3. _____

   _____

Think Think
Think Th
Think Th
Think T
Think Thi
Think T
Think Th
Think

Think Think
Think Think
Think
Think Think
Think Think
Think
Think Think
Think
Think Think

When Jake felt "jumpy" he had his mind on a million and one things. He was usually very excited and had a hard time concentrating on one thing at a time. Sometimes this made Jake forgetful and he'd lose things that were important, like his homework, the keys to his house, his wallet, his library books...even his watch!

Can you help Jake find the five things that he lost? Circle them in the picture below. (The answers are on page 55).

As Jake learned to "settle down" he learned to be better organized. He made a list of the things that he needed to take with him every day and he kept them in a shoe box on his dresser. Make a list of the things that you need to have every day. Can you think of one place where you can keep them?

THINGS I NEED EVERYDAY

_____

_____

_____

_____

_____

_____

_____

_____

_____

Jake's counselor, Ms. Simon, taught him another way to remember things that were important. It is called "mnemonics" (pronounced new-mon-ics). Ms. Simon said, "Mnemonics is a kind of trick to help you remember things. A lot of very smart people use this trick to help them learn all kinds of things. One mnemonic trick is to make a sentence out of words that have the first letter of the things that you have to remember. It is easier for the mind to remember something that make sense, like a sentence, than to remember each thing by itself. If the sentence is funny, or has a rhyme in it, then it is easier to remember.

Here is the sentence that Jake made up to remember to take his keys, his wallet, his watch, and his homework—every day.

<u>K</u>ids <u>w</u>ill <u>w</u>ant <u>h</u>oney.

Can you think of another sentence using the same first letters?

K_____

w_____

w_____

h_____

Make a list of some things that you have to remember. Then make up a sentence using the first letters. How funny can you make the sentence?

50

As Jake learned to settle down, everybody seemed to treat him better and better. His mom was always smiling at him, his teacher would pat him on the head, and his friends seemed to always want to be with him. Jake wondered, "Do people really like to be with me more now that I have settled down? Or did I settle down because people were so nice to me and I wanted to do something nice for them? Which came first, the chicken or the egg?"

Well, Jake didn't know which came first. What do you think? How about the things listed below? Put a "1" by the things that you think came first and a "2" by the things that you think followed. (The answers are on page 55).

When Jake thought about it, the most important thing that he learned about settling down was to THINK about things before he did them. He found that when he thought things out, he was more likely to do them right the first time. Can you THINK of the ways that Jake might have changed?

Here is a list of the "old" ways that Jake did things. Write below each one the way that you THINK Jake does them now.

WHEN JAKE HAD TO BUY A PRESENT FOR SOMEONE HE'D GET THEM WHATEVER HE WOULD LIKE.

_____

WHEN JAKE DIDN'T KNOW AN ANSWER ON HIS HOMEWORK, HE WOULD JUST GUESS AT IT.

_____

WHEN JAKE COULDN'T FIND SOMETHING RIGHT AWAY, HE WOULD JUST MAKE AN EXCUSE ABOUT LOSING IT.

_____

WHEN JAKE DID SOMETHING WRONG, HE WOULD BLAME IT ON SOMEONE ELSE.

_____

_____

When Jake grew up, his wish came true. He had worked so hard and won so many friends and became such a sensible I-can-do-it kind of frog that he got his wish. Do you remember what it was? If you don't, there's a hint in Jake's lunch. Take the first letter of each food on this page and then put the letters in order to find out. (The answer is on page 55).

Draw a picture of what you want to be when you're grown up. Then fold it up, place it in a cardboard box, and bury it. Come back in 20 years and dig it up to see if you were right!

ANSWERS

page 14 - Thinking of a peaceful and relaxing place, counting to 10 slowly, taking a hot bath, taking deep breaths.

page 15 - Top: muddy frog prints on floor, clothes all over room, toys not picked up, TV left on, plate of food left on floor.
Bottom: clean clothes on clothesline, dishes washed and stacked on counter, table set, playroom straightened up.

page 19 - Jake in circus, monster scaring Jake, alligator eating Jake's homework, alien kidnapping Jake.

page 20 - Radio (could make it hard for Jake to concentrate), paint jars (could spill all over Jake's homework), toy soldiers (might distract Jake from his homework), drink (could spill all over the desk).

page 21 - TEN commandments, meat TENderizer, TENnis balls, TEN dollar bill, TEN cents (dime), TENt

page 26 - Enemy: TV, video games, toy chest, candy bars, telephone, radio.
Good Guys: Desk calendar, clock, dictionary, file folders, homework chart, chores chart.

page 28 - Here are a few things that Jake could have done: piled up bricks and stones to give him more height; make a see-saw using an old board, and throw a stone to catapult him over; make a lasso with the rope, throw it around of the tree and pull himself over.

page 31 - Stamps, miniatures, buttons, bugs, coins, plants.

page 33 - I'M SORRY!

page 35 - Teacher, grandmother, father, friend, principal, mother, uncle.

page 37 - Room is messy, junk food is all over the place, radio is blaring, bed is unmade, desk is a mess, clock on wall is broken.

page 39 - TALK IT OUT

page 42 - Trucks are sorted by size; shirts are folded on bed by pattern; encyclopedia on bookshelf is sorted by alphabet; "To Do" list on wall is sorted by number; sports equipment is organized by activity: baseball and glove, hockey stick and puck.

page 44 - Jake getting out of bed, Jake putting on socks, Jake putting on shoes, Jake eating breakfast, Jake washing breakfast dishes, Jake walking out door and waving good-bye.

page 45 - Slowly: taking a test, doing homework, choosing from a menu, trying to figure out which direction to go.
Quickly: playing basketball, riding a bicycle in the street.

page 48 - Pencil in chair, books under bed, watch in plant, homework under plant, keys in glass of water.

page 51 - 1: Jake studying, 2: Paper with an "A." 1: Jake doing the dishes, 2: Mother giving Jake a cupcake.
1: Jake washing car, 2: Father giving Jake his allowance. 1: Jake buying a present, 2: Jake going to a party.

page 53 - <u>M</u>ilk, <u>A</u>pple, <u>Y</u>ogurt, <u>O</u>range, <u>R</u>aisins.

About the Author:

Lawrence E Shapiro, Ph.D. has had more than fifteen years working with children as a teacher, school psychologist, director of a school for special-needs children, and in private practice. He is the author of eight books and has invented over fifteen psychological games. Dr. Shapiro is the catalog president of Childswork/Childsplay, the country's largest distributor of psychologically oriented toys, games, and books based in Plainview, New York.

About the Illustrator:

Reggie Byers has made inroads in the comic book industry with his Jam Quacky series of independently-produced comic books featuring multicultural animal heroes. His artwork has appeared in magazines and rap videos. He lives in Philadelphia.